It's game day morning,
I leap from bed,
My gear's all ready, full steam ahead!

Breakfast done,
My teeth shine bright,
Ready to play and feel just right!

We circle up, our voices shout, This is the game we've dreamed about!

We skate and pass, we stretch and slide, With every move, we build our stride.

My legs feel tired, my breath runs thin, But I push hard — I won´t give in!

The puck is mine, my teammates cheer,
This is our moment, the win is near!

The goalie snags it with his glove,
What a save — a stop to love!

I shoot my shot — it finds its way,
We win the game — what a day!

Orange slices, stories too,
We laugh and cheer—
our team came through!

Pancakes for dinner — what a treat,
A winning day feels extra sweet!